ONE HUNDRED POEMS FOR HEARING DOGS

In support of

Hearing Dogs for Deaf People

Various Authors

Edited by Mel Wardle Woodend

Illustrated by Louise Jutton

ONE HUNDRED POEMS FOR HEARING DOGS

First Printing: 2025

Typeset in Arial 8/10/11/16/28 by Dream Well Writing Ltd

Printed and bound by Amazon UK

ISBN: 97817394900-96 (DREAM WELL WRITING)

DREAM WELL WRITING LTD

STAFFORDSHIRE

UNITED KINGDOM

www.dreamwellwriting.simplesite.com

A Dyslexia Friendly Publication

An anthology of poetry written by dog lovers to celebrate our woofy canine companions and raise money for Hearing Dogs for Deaf People. These poems will capture the hearts of everybody who has ever been lucky enough to have and love a dog....

This anthology has been produced in support of Hearing Dogs for Deaf People. The poems contained within are not the views of the charity but are the views expressed by the writers.

Dedication

To all the Hearing, Sound Support, and Confidence and Companion Dogs who help their deaf partners leave loneliness behind.

Acknowledgements

Thank you to everyone who has taken the time to write and submit poetry for this collection; to Jennifer Brown, Marcello Giovanelli, Maggie Hampton, Gracie Pinson-Bradley, Chris Warnock, and Aaron Wise for helping me with the final selection of poems to include; and to Louise Jutton for her wonderful illustrations and cover artwork.

The biggest thanks, of course, goes to all the dogs: both pet dogs and working dogs who make their humans' lives better every day with joyful tail wags and unconditional love; and a special thank you to all the staff and volunteers who are part of Hearing Dogs for Deaf People charity and who work with the most incredible dogs who go on to change deaf people's lives. These dogs are amazing real-life heroes, who help keep their deaf recipients safe and help them to leave loneliness behind.

Introduction

When I woke one morning in December 2021 with sudden severe hearing loss, my world changed overnight. I had been fully hearing for the first forty-one years of my life so adapting to hearing loss and a subsequent related health condition was (and still often is) incredibly challenging. It can be frightening and isolating not being able to hear some of the everyday sounds I used to take for granted.

I joined a lipreading group and the instructor told me about Hearing Dogs for Deaf People. I applied and after a while they found a match for me! Sound Support Dog Kirrie is the most wonderful Miniature Poodle, who is full of mischief, friendly, loving, and so very confident and clever in her sound work alerting me to the everyday sounds I would otherwise miss. She makes my life better in so many ways because I feel safe at home, and out and about with her travelling to university on the train, being with her in the office where she will alert me to the fire alarm should it go off, or travelling to my Mum's house on the bus. I feel safer now with Kirrie walking with me along pavements where I cannot hear people, scooters, or bikes approaching from behind me.

At home, Kirrie alerts me to the alarm clock every day so I do not oversleep. It is wonderful to wake up with her serious face and loving brown eyes gazing into mine. She is very persuasive and won't let me ignore her wake-up alert or go back to sleep! She is brilliant at her work! She is so much fun and she is my reason to get out of bed and go out of the house every day enjoying our life together! Kirrie makes me feel safe because I know when there are sounds at home I might miss such as the doorbell, my phone, and the cooker timer, she will alert me. If my husband or my Mum need me and I am in another room, they ask Kirrie to 'find Mummy!' and she rushes to fetch me with a confident nudge of her nose, from wherever I am in the house. The most important sounds are, of course, the smoke alarm and carbon monoxide detector. Recently, Kirrie alerted me to the carbon monoxide detector sounding in our kitchen at 1.30am. She was fast asleep in her bed when the alarm went off! Luckily it was a faulty alarm and not a leak but if it had been, she would have saved our lives that night!

Everyone at the charity Hearing Dogs for Deaf People works so hard. There are many people involved with each dog: puppy volunteers, trainers, welfare, vets, and the people who work with potential recipients assessing their needs and finding the right match. When a dog and their deaf recipient are matched there is ongoing support with visits from a partnership instructor, medical experts to help answer any queries, and so much more!

I want to be able to do something to raise money for and to raise awareness of Hearing Dogs charity because they have given me the most wonderful gift of Kirrie! As a poet, I thought curating a poetry anthology about dogs would be a great way to do this so here is *One Hundred Poems for Hearing Dogs*! I hope you enjoy it and thank you for your support!

Mel Wardle Woodend

Staffordshire Poet Laureate 2019-2022 and Director of Dream Well Writing Ltd

Sound Support

For Sound Support Dog Kirrie

I give you a hug and a kiss goodnight
and you circle round in your bed curling up tight,
you smell of woolly jumpers
and your fur is just as soft,
jet black curls
with flecks of grey and white.

Conker brown irises
peek out of clear bright white
from under long lashes you watch my every move
as I settle down for the night.

Sometime in the early hours
you wake, stretch and stand
then jump up onto my bed
and light as a feather you land!

I wake up with my arm draped across your curls
and when you feel me moving, a great big yawn unfurls
but it is much too early to rise
so we yawn and we snuggle and we both close our eyes
until I feel a nudge from your strong confident nose
because the alarm clock is going off
and you're telling me it's time to be up and on our toes!

Mel Wardle Woodend

Contents

PART ONE

DOGS

A Midwinter Night's Dream

Stepping off the vaporetto at the Lido,
glancing up into a clear December night
who should I see but Orion with his hounds,
striding out to round up his starry herds of cattle –
and I am six again, sitting on the floor
of the stoep, cushioned between Spartan
and Bell, while the smoke of father's cigarette
drifts overhead.

Black veldt of heaven so pricked, so star studded,
there's scarcely room to put a pin between them –
my father shows me how to find Orion
and his dogs – Look, there's Spartan, there's Bell!
When only six I understood the dogs resting
beside me were also running in the sky.

I had forgotten – now I look up – I see them,
with my father, still rounding up the stars.

Sarah Dale

All Dogs Are Angels

On a silent night
when the mind
explodes
with the cry of
loneliness
four paws tread to
soothe the pain of
emotions.
You won't find
such a depth
in the best
romance,
it only hides
behind their irises.
A great blessing
has come to
humanity,
revealed in dogs,
the angels arrived,
though without
wings.

Norbert Góra

An Ode to Dogs

There are small dogs, tall dogs,
shaggy dogs and waggy dogs,
affable dogs and flappable dogs!

There are grumpy dogs, jumpy dogs,
running dogs and funny dogs,
working dogs and herding dogs too.

There are dogs called Poodles, Labradoodles,
Bloodhounds, Dachshunds,
Dalmatians and even Pomeranians.

But best of all, we surely can agree,
whether a mongrel or a pedigree,
are the ones we love ... love unconditionally.

Helen Torr

Book of Dog

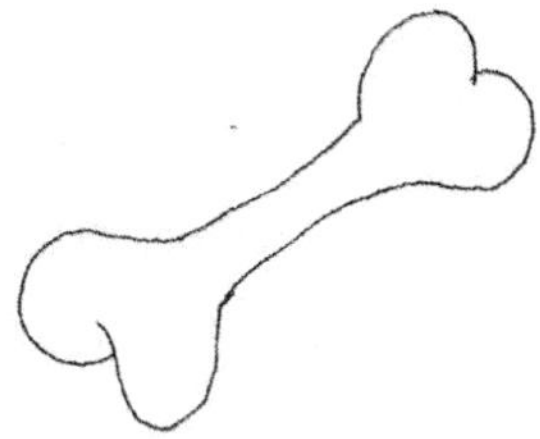

When you find your people, stay!
If they take care of you
take care of them –
loyalty makes them feel good.

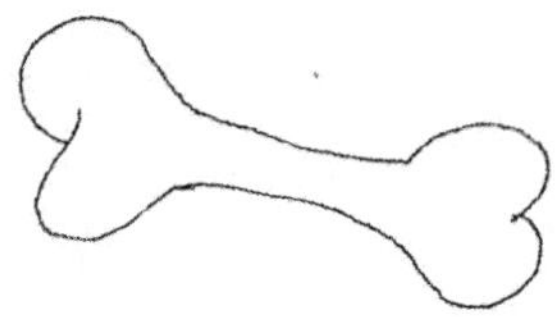

To get what you want, wait!
Focus on their every move
be ready to make your move –
there may be treats involved.

Sleep with one eye open, leave!
no room for missed chances –
to chase cats, cars
squirrels, balls...

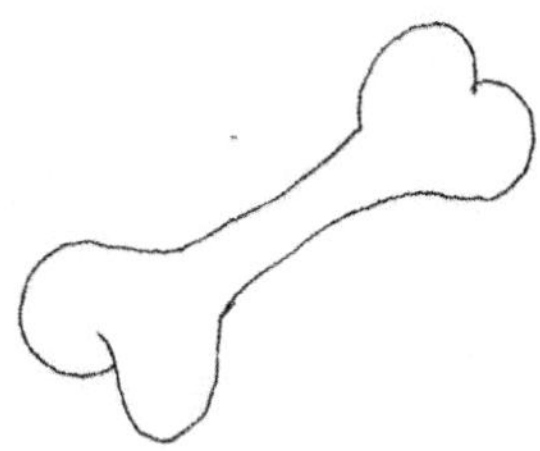

Smell out adventure, find!
rewards in hidden places –
only you know life
is more exciting at the edges.

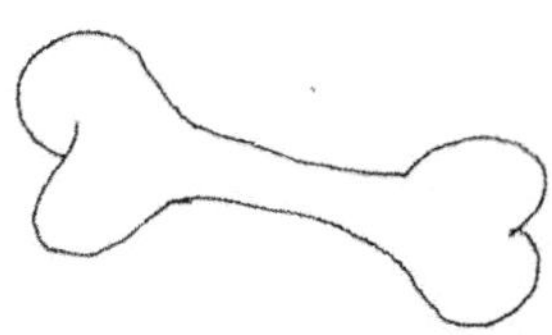

If you're under attack, come!
to a quick decision –
trust your instincts
and follow your nose.

Dawn Jutton

Staffordshire Poet Laureate 2022-2024

Cemetery Dog Walk 1

Draggled by dew, my shoelace unties.
I reknot it to a trim bouquet of loops,
read a headstone. Next stop, I scoop
up dog poo, work out the longest lives.

The bag is so thin I feel the warmth leave,
the way a failing body leaks its heat.
I worry if it's OK for dogs to defecate
on the hearth of the dead, while others grieve.

A stone cross, arms outstretched, grins
approval of my mouthing names as I pass.
It makes them live, heals my own stressing.

My spent offering thuds in the wheelie bin.
I close the lid. The dog's snout parts the grass,
sniffs the breath of a spirit's blessing.

Helen Kay

Cutie

The flat, open space of the heath gives rise
to two elderly people walking dogs.
A small, short haired mongrel, full of whiskers,
dashes away from them towards me,
stops, looks up, blinks his long lashes and smiles,
wagging his stubby tail.
And he waits.

'You're a cutie', I say, straight away
embarrassed at my unusual soppiness.
The owner hobbles over on crutches,
tells me he's a rescue dog she saw
and fell for at the Dogs' Home. 'He's 10
years old. First time off the lead. They told me
he was a sweetie. I'm really pleased with him.
He's rescued me.'

Getting used to my new-found self, I say
'He's so cute; so friendly.' I feel
really pleased for her. 'His name's Julian',
she says and smiles; and I wonder
how many times he's been rescued,
how many times he's rescued others,
in such a short life:

Such a sweet smile, such engaging lashes,
such beautiful eyes. Such soppinesses.

Ron Harper

Days of Loneliness

I sometimes sit
and wonder,
who was the first to let you in?
How many years waiting,
huddled and afraid
in fire-lit caves,
listening to moon-kissed howls that chill
despite the flames' red heat.
Or was it you
who sought us out?
Guided by need or instinct
or some secret desire to belong?
You started as wolves,
that's true,
but look at you now;
guard and guide,
farmer and shepherd,
therapist, companion and friend.
And you have earned a place beside the fire,
and our days of loneliness have come to an end.

Dale Parnell

Dog Graveyard

Mostly with sanctioned joy our dogs
sprinted or trotted the path to where dogs

could roll and snoot through sand, flop in the surf,
or follow us to deep water in a leisurely dog

paddle. Some slipped away quietly,
loping waterward in their stealth dog

mission to check that the lone swimmer
among their pack didn't require a dog

to return her safely to the family gathering
on the patio populated with too many dogs.

Yet others worked harder, pushed
through screens and doors formerly dog-

proofed to careen toward us in a frenzy that frightened
other swimmers. Hey, Michelle! Is that your dog?

This path angling among pines walks us on chips
and soft needles between all the good dogs.

Michelle DeRose

Dogs

Domesticated wolf

Open hearted

Graceful as he runs

Silly as ever

Nephele K. Pinnock (age 8)

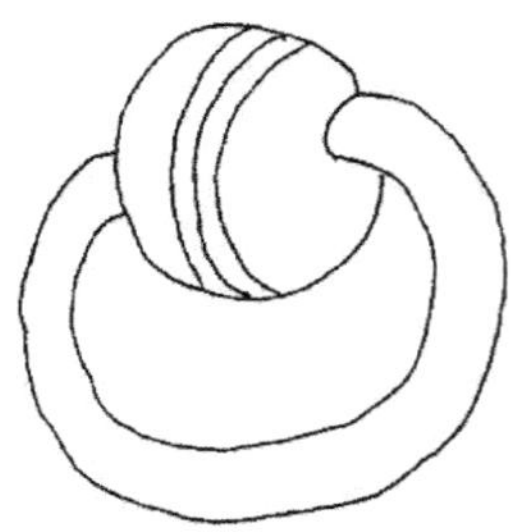

Dogs

Pedigree pooches or Heinz 57
for farmsteads or special support
ones from a shelter or tail-wagging pups
with legs that are gangly or short
long coated, hairless, or wiry or smooth
harness or collars with leads
for walks in the hills or a run in the park
there's a dog to suit everyone's needs

Yvonne Ugarte

Everything They Have

I grew up with
mostly dogs,
and I love them
because they are
loyal and kind;
they get excited when
you're happy and they try to
cheer you up when you're
sad—

they protect you
and love
you always,

I think it's a beautiful thing to
be loved by a dog;

they have nothing to
give you but love and memories
and so they give you both
with everything they have.

Linda M. Crate

Friendship Without End

To write about a dog,
is to write about a friend,
a friend who gives their all,
in a friendship without end.

A world without a dog,
is a dark and silent space,
and a world without a canine friend,
is a strange and empty place.

Many times, I've heard it said,
'A dog is man's best friend.'
A sobriquet so very true,
in a friendship without end...

Graham Cawser

Juno and the Fire

She'll never understand
why her beloved man
lays then lights the logs
that pop and blaze. She lives
to warn against all terror,
tries to lead the way
to basement safety. If not there,
than anywhere away
from here–far kitchen corners,
behind a sturdy chair.
Meanwhile, the cat moves close,
ignores its crackling evil.
You cannot trust a fire.
You can't trust tabbies, either.

Michelle DeRose

Let sleeping dogs lie

in the middle of your beds,
on hot afternoon patios, in all
the major household thoroughfares;
in halls, and on the stairs,
under tables, around chairs,
even on the futon no one ever wants to sleep on.

Let them mime-dream on carpets
magic-ed into grass and endless beaches,
chasing shadows over land and sandscapes,
mouthing their pleasures and excitements.

Let them live each wild, joyous walk again,
in the breaks from guarding home and humans;
for them, there's no drowsy interlude between sleep and waking.

Let them lie, not still, not silent,
sometimes even open-eyed, ideally at your side:
you, substitute litter-mate, ear scratcher
and a valued source of heat.

Ali Rowland

Man's Best Friend

The love of dogs. Oft regarded as man's best friend,

Always pleased to see you, never let you down,

A joy to share, a helping hand,

Ever present, with you all the way.

A dog is ever faithful, on which you can rely,

A special friend, a different friend,

With talents of their own,

There to help and guide you, protecting you from harm.

Dogs sense danger, illness and vulnerability,

They can warn you. They can indicate what they mean without words,

They can stand in for your senses or add some of their own,

With loyalty and faithfulness, they can act on your behalf.

Show them love and care for them, is all that they require,

For years of willing service, there by your side,

They will get to know your meaning, your character and mood,

They will look to help and support you, in many different ways.

Chris Boult

Murphy's Morning Movie

Each sniff unspools from overhanging hedge
a wealth of footage snagged amongst the twigs.
Each leaf reports some rumor's tasty edge
and scent by scent the news in nostril swigs
is slurped into the canine's avid head.

A connoisseur of stretching every whiff
from short subject to full-fledged featurette,
he ambles poking on his way unmiffed
by owner's urgent tugs upon his leash.
Tail up or down is how he rates the show.

He's quite the ardent fan of each release
that plays across the widescreen of his nose.
Of senses it's the main one left – his sight
and hearing cut to get the movie right.

John Newsom

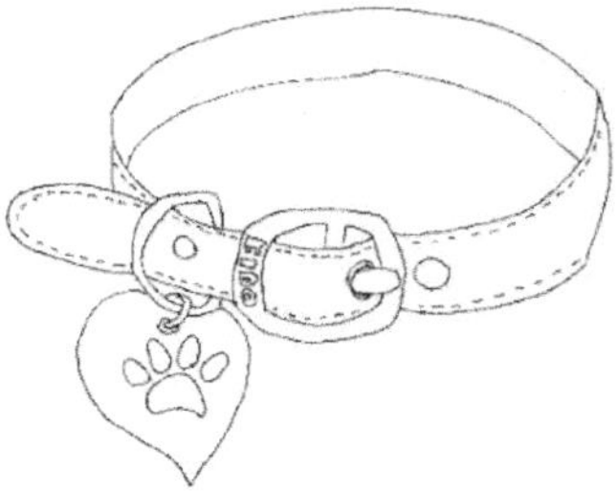

My Faithful Friend

A present for a girl called Suzy,
who was often very choosy.
Her present was a dog called Bert,
and their friendship was a real cert.

He looked after her night and day,
she could not hear but he liked to play.
Her mummy said he was a dog so cute,
and they would make a very good suit.

Bert is trained to alert Suzy if something arose,
by giving her a nudge with his cold wet nose.
Then place his little paw upon her lap
to draw attention to the little chap.

It was a picture of Berty in the local news.
And he was chewing his owner's shoes.

Timothy P. Stavert

My Friend Had a Fall

An unmapped walk with Morag,
her Golden Labrador. I had a text
for help. I trust the dog's sniffing
scents to guide my way along
these terraces that ribbon the hill:
there's Lewis Street
and Lewis Lewis street;
there's South Williams Street
and North Williams Street;
Jones Street and Ivor Road.
There's no tugging, no hurry.
A bag-laden shopper, with child,
the latter pats Morag's head. I share
a friendly dog-owner smile.
She's called 'Morag' I say.

There's a kissing gate at the end
of Ivor Road, it opens onto a flat field.
Morag is nearly twelve,
though the lead is patterned
with puppies, she seems forever
young with her waggy tail
and runs with a barking joy.
I throw her ball. I take a photograph
to share with my friend.

Phil Wood

Read-Aloud

I needed to read the end of the story
before we got there—
the two of us
side-by-side in the empty room,
backs against the wall, me reading out loud,
each of us sure the dog would die.
At eight, he couldn't bear it, already weeping
with what he knew would happen,
and how it could not be borne.
He didn't want to know.
I didn't want to know either, but stories
need endings   and it was my job
to get us there, each with our bruised heart,
beginning life without his father:
a dilapidated rental with worn carpet;
uneven doorframes; folding chairs
and a card table in the kitchen.
Pocket change for milk.
So while he wept, I read ahead,
found that the dog—against all odds—
survives.
It's okay, I told him then.
It's okay. We can keep going. And we did.

Laura Apol

Remembering Bruno

Time's iron hand has slipped your collar, loosed your leash–
you're free now, still running in some other wood;
entrancing symphonies of smells, quivering tail
expressing all joy, ears pricked to hear the voice
that calls you home – each day a bright new world.

Sarah Dale

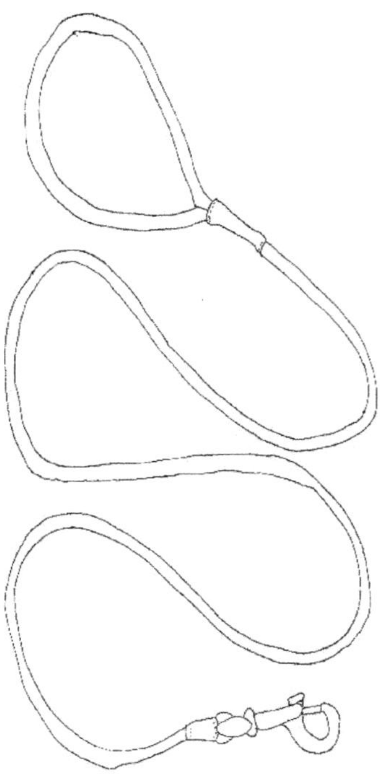

Summer Meadow

Time for dogs to stroll,
as sun beats shade in cedar.
Beneath feet, tunnels mole
while insects follow-my-leader.

The dogs don't play the game,
they raise an eye, a brow,
'Don't care' they sniff, declaim,
'it's too hot anyhow.'

White umbels hum and hover,
alien crafts dip and tower
above grasses' itchy pother,
and burdock in full flower.

Two Yorkies find their spring
over green and prickly blades,
they almost seem to sing
in a momentary patch of shade.

Summer echoes heard,
warm drowsing summer words,
calls of birds are slurred,
dogs doze, droop, demur.

Polly Stretton

The Drink

June bugs jitterbugging on the puppy's bowl
summon summer moonbeams as they rock and roll.

Poodle pup, while lapping, bumps into the brim.
June bugs, puddle paddling, learn to do the Swim.

Helen Zax

The Little Black Dog

The house stood empty, soft dust-snow drifting on invisible air.

And in the darkest shadowed corner,

the little black dog waited.

Years folded into years.

Like the pages of a thick, ancient book.

And she sat, not breathing, not seeing, not hearing.

A ghost, waiting for her young master to grow weary,

to finish his long life and lie in peace.

She would wait, and walk with him again,

and one day, he came to the door.

Dared to search, just… in case.

And there, curled in the gloom, almost invisible,

shadow on shadow.

Velvet ears pleated,

the same deep blackberry eyes, full now of a quiet joy.

Good girl, he whispered. *You're here!*

Small tail, thumping in the dust.

A walk!

Out of the house, the gloom, the shadows.

The cool spring world holding still.

A finger of dawn gleamed, reaching down to them.

One last walk.

Carolyn Ward

The Offering

She can't make herself any smaller;
the wall can't embrace her any closer.
A hand is raised,
she cowers,
she waits
for the blow to fall.

Instead of strike there is stroke.

A voice,
calm, not shouting;
words never heard before,
'good girl.'
Another hand held out;
in its palm
something her empty stomach
yearns for,
just as her leaking teats
ache for the suckle of her pups.
Dare she?
The voice continues to calm,
the hand continues to stroke.
She accepts the offering.

Marilyn Pemberton

The Staffordshire Way

Ears fall softly
like velvet drapery,
framing the slowly
broadening valley of
your Staffordshire landscape.
Many shades clothe
your shifting form –
blue/grey as the silvery sky,
inhaled whilst watching
passing silhouettes
dip and soar,
tortoiseshell like the moist autumn mulch
that carpets your brindle, bridle way
stirring snuffling nostrils.
Until one day
the final contours of
your heart-shaped head
and broadly beaming smile
slip into place.
Bull terrier by name
loving and loyal
is the Staffordshire way.

Kathy Dowling

Wolves don't howl at the moon

they only raise their head,
to allow them to be better heard,
so their word can be spread.

Haven't you ever had a dog,
that lies beneath a roof,
and howls when there is no moon?
That alone should be proof.

Gareth Barsby

Wordless Befriender

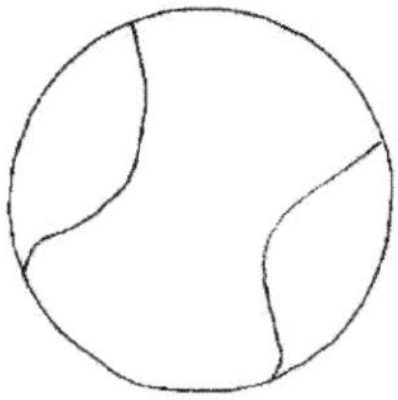

Joyful greeter
puller of socks off my feet-er
comforting routine-er
little portal to places greener
tail chasing spinner
hopeful black nose near my dinner
unconditional presence
living and breathing anti-depressant
leftovers hoover-er
nervous system soother-er
wordless befriender
sofa corner defender
in-the-moment grounder
a calmness around her
the embodiment of blessed
my continuous invitation to rest

Ange Disbury

PART TWO

CLEVER DOGS, DAFT DOGS!

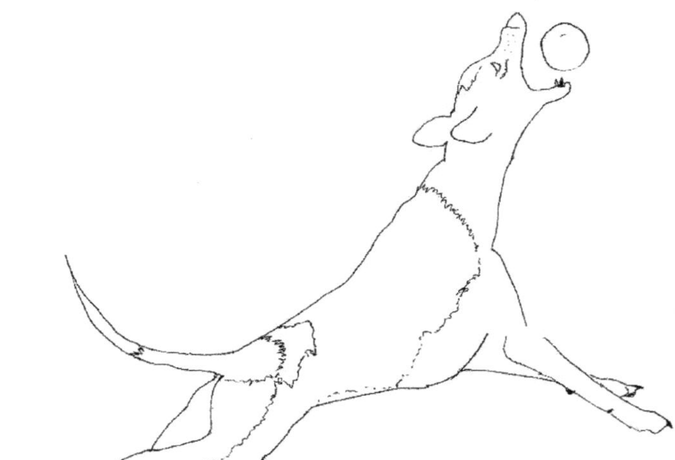

'Mayhem', the Lurcher

Pup of the noble Finbar and some friendly mutt,
she bounds into each day with glossy glee,
ebony eel on carbon fibre springs,
an ecstasy of life.

Ripped books,
wrecked chairs,
trashed shoes or scattered bin –
low as a snake she hugs the floor,
holding her breath.

An impish peep from chip of gleaming jet,
and the mirth of her,
the lanky, leaping joy of her,
the, shining prancing bliss of her,
save her.

Anne Picken

The Pet Shower

Winner of Birmingham Dogs Home poetry competition 2020

It rained cats and dogs last night
and my lawn is no longer green,
every space is filled with animals;
a soggy pet-filled scene.

A Bulldog's crying in a puddle,
a Tabby is tickling a Pug,
a Whippet is lying sideways
giving a Burmese a hug.

A Setter drinks from a bird bath,
he's splashing a Borzoi nearby;
she's strutting away with elegance
holding her head up high.

A Beagle's tormenting worms,
a St Bernard's high-fiving a Manx,
an Afghan's looking outraged
at their silly child-like pranks.

A Persian's trying to breaststroke,

but it seems to be more of a crawl;
Sparrows stare in amazement
and give all their friends a call.

Today's dawn chorus is strange;
I've never heard the like before,
with meows and woofs all competing
as I clear all the muck from my door.

Janet Jenkins

Dogged Expression

Who says dogs don't have memories?
People who don't have dogs.
If you live with canine hoodlums
you see an ability to recognise words,
know their instant recall,
except when you call them to come back.

Yet, say 'walk' or 'dinner' when they're not around
and they appear
tails wagging, ears pricked,
as if to say, 'what, did I miss something?'
with that enquiring look
so familiar to those lucky enough
to be looked after
by little hoodlums
like mine.

Polly Stretton

Investigating the Park

This may come as a surprise to you
as your nose is as useful as a chocolate teapot,
but there's a smell over there we must pursue.
So if you don't mind, we could go to that spot
the one by the big old tree where we all pee.
You know the one.
I understand there's other spots you want to explore
but this is one thing that I can't ignore.
And if evolution hadn't failed you, you'd agree with me!
I'm not the one being disagreeable—
I might be pulling like crazy but I'm not unstable—
I'm not the one spending all day sitting at the table—
I'm trying to show you interesting things outside!
Ahah, I've convinced you. We're heading over
and there you can see - a pigeon has died.
Isn't the world wonderful, isn't it wide?
Isn't this pack of gum just curious
isn't the park so mysterious?
Let's stay here forever - let's see the world!
Now look over there-there's a bird—

Kelsie Colclough

Joy's a Thing With Flapping Ears

After Emily Dickinson

Joy's a thing with flapping ears –
A tail that windmills free –
A wriggling bum – a lolling tongue –
A furry yap of glee.

And even when I'm feeling glum –
It says – just look around!
A stick! – or mud! – can stir the blood –
Fun's waiting to be found.

It's often at my heels – and then –
It goes elsewhere to play –
But always – it comes bounding back –
Joy's never far away.

Sarah Ziman

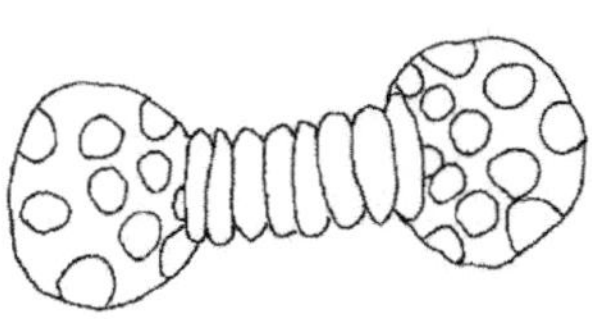

Not Everything Is Food

You really are quite peculiar,
have a really strange attitude.
You seem to think, everything you find
has to be some kind of food.

Well I must say, it's not normal
when you're walking down a street,
to think everything on the pavement
has been left for you to eat.

In the park you snuffle everywhere
with only one thing on your mind,
determined to make a doggy meal
out of anything that you find.

To you, things looks so delicious,
you have no taste buds, it would seem,
I'm amazed at what you consider
to be the height of hound cuisine.

Even at home you never stop,
you're always nosing around,
you know, it doesn't have to be food

just ‘cus it’s been left on the ground.

I’ve seen you eat sticks, flowers and grass,
all shapes and colours of poo,
you must get indigestion because
most things, you don’t even chew.

You have a wide and varied diet,
there’s nothing you won’t exclude,
but it’s really time you understood
not everything you find is food!

Mogs

Sitting on the Kitchen Floor in Your Way at 5pm

My humans who I love so dearly,
I understand the bond you have so clearly!
No hurdle or fence is too big to jump,
together you've faced swerving roads and bumps, but

not even Hardknott Pass could rock the boat
or maybe it did, I wouldn't know, I
was busy barking at goats.

Please read back the first letter of each line to see what I want the most. The packet is literally on that counter there. It's OK, I can wait.

Kelsie Colclough

Sonnet of Apology to the Postman

You stroll up the driveway and the barking has started,
you already know what you're going to meet-
you're exploring, carefully, the uncharted
of riverbed pebbles under your feet.
Calmly, you sift through a bag of life,
and retrieve an envelope with a little rush.
At the letterbox there's gnawing teeth with strife,
you ponder before you begin to push
the letter through the door.
Then you hear the shredding and a telling off,
as paper rains upon a wooden floor;
it's followed by a heavy scoff.
You walk away, you managed to survive-
you're back in your van and ready to drive.

Harry Fletcher

Staffordshire Young Poet Laureate 2024-2025

The Day of the Dog Show Rebellion

As is often the case with uprisings no one can fully recall

where the flashpoint came from, as surely it did and dog voices were raised round the hall.

'We will not be judged' cried Afghans and Airedales, Bulldogs snorted 'Indeed we protest!'

And the Beagles joined in, as Beagles are wont to, by eating the yellow rosettes.

The Collies collected the tweed-skirted judges and rounded them up in the vestry

where a Miniature Dachshund kept them in check, skilled by his snappy ancestry.

English Setters, French Bulldogs and big German Shepherds gave 'Woof' and a 'Wuf' and a 'Ouaf'

whilst a Hamilton Hound twirled around and around. (He's from Sweden and known as Olaf.)

There went up a cheer. 'The Irish are here!' The Wolfhound, the Setter and Terrier

gave a tuneful rendition of old Danny boy, Jack Russell on flute, on accordion big LeonBerger.

An Old English Sheepdog led the appaws whilst the Poodle, the Peke and the Pug

stood on their tiptoes and threw out their chests like their friend - a Rottweiler called Thug.

Now a Staffie stepped onto the silverwared stage. 'We've had it with all these dog shows.

We refuse to be judged by the gait of our limbs, the length of our ears and the size of our front and back paws.'

'Hear hear' piped the Silky, the Toy Fox, the Vizsla. 'We are more than the sum of our parts.'

'If you really must judge' sang the Wei-Wei-Weimeraner, 'just look at the size of our hearts.'

'We are faithful and loyal!' said a Westie, 'Our hearts full of love to the brim.'

'Well up to a point but don't go overboard' said a bolshie young Whippet named Jim.

They cracked into the snacks and the dog gravy ales, Yorkshire Terriers running the bar

and the news of the dog-show rebellion on socials has made them all media stars.

It's been quite a day in a pawsitive way. Now there's just the odd snore, fart and sigh.

Sssh. Let's creep away as they dream their dog dreams. It's time to let sleeping dogs lie.

Jane King

The Dog Chorus

To the tune of 'The Frog Chorus'

It's getting dark,
let's have a lark,
let's have a howl, a whimper and bark,
we're all shut out,
wandering about,
so we all bark together.

No matter the time,
a singing canine,
sits in the garden, in the moonshine.
We yap and we howl,
we snarl and we growl,
then we all bark together.

People complain,
say we're a pain,
they say they can't sleep, and that we're to blame,
they don't think it's right
that all through the night
we all bark together.

Mogs

W-A-L-K

Our drowsy dog seems fast asleep,
with one eye open just a peep,
so all is calm until I say
W-A-L-K!

A sudden yelp, a boisterous blur,
a doggie dance of feet and fur,
careering, veering, to and fro!
Come on, you humans, don't be slow!
I've got my ball, it's time to go!

She's out the door and hurtling free:
a surge of pent-up energy!
She hares and tears and leaps and larks,
and celebrates in joyful barks.
She thrives outside: with sparkling eyes,
she chases passing butterflies,
and races after ball or stick –
a catch mid-air's her favourite trick.

She tracks the smells along the trail,
with twitching ears and thumping tail,
then capers in the meadow flowers.

Her paws won't pause for hours and hours!

She's wild for wildlife, fun and play.

There's *nothing* else that makes her day

like *W-A-L-K*!

Claire Schlinkert

Whipplington

I’m being watched by a Whipplington
lying on his comfy bed ‘asleep’.
Pretending to be good
as he knows he really should
but in the depth of ‘slumber’ he can keep
a watchful eye on food that I am eating.
That lively Lurcher’s brain is wide awake
for the moment when
he can rise up from his den
to eat the crust he knows that he can take.

A ‘Whipplington’ is a cross between a Whippet and a Beddlington Terrier.

Francis Charters

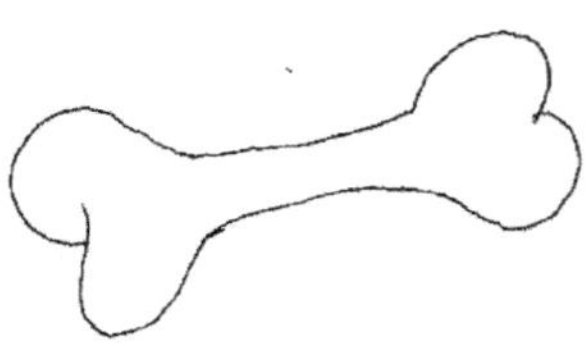

You Good Dog You

My dog ran off with a total stranger, happily climbed
in his pickup truck, with nary a glance behind.
I threw her clothes on the sidewalk –
that little green number I found at Saks,
the blue sailor suit – aww, she looked so cute.

Fluffy and Spike ran rough down the coast,
knocked off six or 7-11s, outsmarted the guard at PetSmart,
always making a clean getaway
like Warren Beatty and Faye Dunaway,
her head out the window brazenly barking.

Holed up in some flea-bag motel, a ratfink cat
ratted them out. Police surrounded them screaming,
Come out! Keep your paws in the air!

Worthless old Spike he copped a plea – the bitch set me up.
The judge he agreed, sent Fluff up the river
for 14 years – to her more like 98.

She shared a cell with a sadistic Shih Tzu,
pumped iron in the prison yard,

sharpened her teeth like a buzz saw,

'til the night of the howling moon

Fluffy managed to chew her way through the bars.

The prodigal pooch pawed at my door, badly needing a bath

and shampoo, preferably one with a fresh citrus scent.

I took her in, because that's what I do.

I told her to stay, and that's what she did.

Jim Smith

PART THREE

MY DOG

'Finbar', the Greyhound

He walks weightless,
a fragile puppet on ethereal strings;
head arrowed down, ears close in velvet folds,
light as indifferent kisses
his claws pitter on pavement.
But haunches swell above the needle legs
and a smooth thickness slabs his neck.

If he walked in wildness he might suddenly
stop, stiffen,
ears sprung to aerials, eyes to lasers.
Then he'd dip… aim… and flash like rippling light,
fly marsh and heather,
fly bracken and bilberry,
bunch-stretch-bunch and swerve with pitiless power
till snarling daggers gash,
race and gash,
and the wide-eyed leaping deer
comes crashing down.

We take him to the park
and try to get him to chase a ball.

Anne Picken

'It's not good news I'm afraid'

He lay on a sheepskin rug. Evaporated.

I look him squarely in the eyes, no hiding from this, my duty is implicit.

I breathe him in, caress his sculpture, cannula linking us to our life thereafter.

A sharp saluting wag of tail. Eyes turn from light to dark; shine to glaze. I close your eyes. I breathe you in.

I'll lie in that hollow of the big tree where the crows call and wait for you.

No longer of this world, we'll walk through long drifting grasses; lift our heads to the lark and into the half light.

Francesca Wheeler

A Dog for All Seasons

This is my dog.
My Tess.
My true companion.
A dog for all seasons,
my all-weather friend.
My big black dog,
with a big brave heart,
who came home to say goodbye.
Thank you Tessy, Pookie, Sweepie, Tessywoo,
(you were all of those names to me).
My Tess,
sleep well in the garden that you loved,
looking out over those fields where you roamed
may your spirit chase frisbees forever.
Precious love.
Ever my friend,
loyal and faithful and sweet,
the best of the best.
Ah, Tess,
walk with me forever Tess,
be always at my side.

Alison Hramiak

A Therapist Tells My Grown Son It's Okay to Experience Joy

All that boy wished for was a dog—a stuffed dog,
dalmatian puppy named Lucky. He'd learned

not to ask for much, not to want, a lesson
I thought would serve him well. The year before,

someone insisted he see Santa. Brave enough
to sit on Santa's lap, he knew the answer

when asked if he'd been good. But when asked
what he wanted, he was perplexed.

By the time he wished for Lucky,
he knew the strength of desire and how to voice it.

Trusted me to hear. Until I told him no—no luck,
no Lucky. Can't always get what you want.

He didn't know I'd told his grandmother,
who bought the spotted puppy with the shiny eyes

and I wrapped it from her. Opening that package
Christmas morning, he was pure delight. I caught it

on film, but photo-taker is all I was—me, the mother
who'd failed him when at last he'd found the words

for want, had risked desire. And Lucky: just a lesson
in caprice. I kept that dog for years after he

left home, but now it's gone, likely gathering dust
in a Goodwill store

in some far-away state
where we used to live.

Laura Apol

A Walk into Autumn's End

Trailing along a countryside path,
amongst an ombre of autumnal shades.
We watch a stream which cascades
memories. I listen to the birdsong,
whilst you try and tug me along.
Then a squirrel jumps out
and you begin to jolt about.
Your softening bark dissipates
into the vastness of the wind-
the squirrel has gone.
You retrieve a freshly fallen
twig- from the squirrel.
A robin flutters by briefly calling.
Your tail wags frantically
as a sudden spurt of teary rain
falls, then stops… replaced by
angelic leaves- each shade
evokes a sense of somethingness,
the path begins to end
and we leave behind our memoria,
hoping to return next autumn.

Harry Fletcher

Staffordshire Young Poet Laureate 2024-2025

An Owner, Who Adores Their Dog

We walk along the pavement;
it has been a busy day.
I listen to your little feet patter,
as you try to keep up with me.
The lead is tangled around my
wrist, I unknot the tangle, knowing
you'll help me along.
Soon enough, we are home and fed,
then snuggled on the sofa with
a blanket. But it's your mottled
coat that keeps me warm.
You sniff my neck and I can smell
essences of freshly cut grass-
your pale blue eyes a summer sky,
which overlooks a wildflower meadow.
When it rains and it feels too cold,
I know I have you to keep me warm.
And when the rain clouds cast a gloom
in the window, I look at your eyes
and it's summer then autumn.
Our favourite time to stroll along,
crunching leaves, in the breezy air.

Harry Fletcher

Staffordshire Young Poet Laureate 2024-2025

At 5am

At 5am the cat arrives, damp
from night-time showers
fresh from wild-kill bowers.

Stealthy, he swings up past the lamp,
lands heavily on the bed,
jumps nimbly across my head,
thankfully, settles down,
gratefully, deep into a purr,
stretches, sleeps, the merest blur
on my dim dreaming.

The dog wakes, joins the cat on the bed
stretches languorously
settles down magnanimously,
lapses into a snoring slumber,
limbs jerking in a dreaming lumber
cumbering the coverlet with the heavy clog
of night-time dog.

At 6am an owl hoots.
The cat still drowses
but the dog, of course, rouses,
they are (not yet) in cahoots.

Dog has a vigorous scratch

slurping over that troublesome patch
snorts hard and attempts to combobulate,
gets me to accept my inevitable fate
and get out of bed to make
the morning pets' collation.

They are definitely in cahoots now
and to make sure I bow
to their need for me to kow-tow
and serve up their chow
the cat utters a plangent meow:
a lambent salutation,
a beneficent oblation

a bed emptying displacement
and I am up and following orders.

Though still dark
the day's arc
has begun.

Dog and cat are one
and have won;
both clever arousers
and I am up and pondering:
who is wearing the trousers?

Stephen Chappell

Basenji Princess of the Upper East Side

Sole queen of the East Side, so aloof and so shy, we
couldn't believe it, it must be a lie!
'Doesn't play well with others,' their note simply said. Yet
you look so royal lounging on your bed.
You accepted our pats and our fawning admiration. Who
knew life with you would have such duration?

Twelve years and counting, you still hold our heart. You
position yourself like a rare piece of art.
Quietly hunting in search of the sun, suspicious of all
frivolity and fun.
Oh, Alibi, you cat-deer-dog, don't pretend you can't hear
me and lay like a log!

We love you dearly, despite all your quirks. Your quiet
demeanor is one of your perks.
You are ladylike, and so sweet to cuddle, but your anger at
other dogs is never subtle.
Why do you hate them with all of your might? Why always
ready for a scissor-kick fight?

You're the prettiest dog we've ever known, and our love for
you has grown and grown.
You curl yourself up like a cinnamon bun, circumnavigating
the house to follow the sun.
Your wardrobe is stylish and your beauty well known.
You've taken ninja quietness to a whole new zone.

You're a sweet little cuddle bug who simply craves pets.
Life with this princess is as good as it gets!

Maggie D. Brace

Bella

She likes the noises in the house
the coming and the going.
She likes the noises in the house
the toing and the froing.

She likes to feel the morning
breeze - the air that blows
through open doors.
She likes to feel the morning
breeze that sweeps her fur and
shakes her paws.
She likes to sleep, it's sleep that's
best. In places where she lays
her head.
She likes to sleep, it's sleep that's
best. She naps like all the
world's her bed.
She likes the noises in the house
the coming and the going.
She likes the noises in the house
the toing and the froing.

Michelle Richardson

Best Friend!

My emotionally supportive, personal trainer,
the gentle, whining alarm that rouses with blackmail and guilt,
the mute, listening ear for the children's anxieties,
our 24/7 intruder prevention system.

The conversation starter on footpaths, in woods,
a magnet for brave toddlers who pat and prod,
the flattener of wheat and crop-circle maker
when zoomies take hold on summer walks.

The entertainer when friends come round,
the most expensive waste disposal money can buy,
the bane of the vacuum cleaner's existence
the shedder of golden hair and painter of rugs.

the beggar of cuddles and manipulator of looks,
the love of the family, we didn't know we needed,
the soul that means you're never alone,
the puppy we welcomed and the old lady yet to come.

Jo Hillman

Bestie

My bestie wears a tartan coat
woven with a MacKenzie check.
A red kerchief about his throat
with tattooed collar on his neck.

My bestie drools on meaty chunks
his favoured sweets, chocolate drops.
A biscuit in his drink he dunks
then to his bed, well-fed he flops.

My bestie, a rapid runner
many rosettes adorn his clothes.
There is no one who is funner
or rubs a cheek on my wet nose.

My bestie is completely loyal
he fends off bullies and my foes.
Treats me as though I am a royal
and strokes my back so I can doze.
My bestie - the best in the world
he gives me cuddles and kisses.
So, have you my puzzle unfurled?
YOU'RE the bestie of my wishes.

Kathryn Beevor

Brushing My Dog's Teeth

I do it every other night
so that he doesn't dread it
as a fixed routine.

I put a blob of liver-flavoured
toothpaste on two finger-brushes
and stand them upright
on the dressing table.

He's on the bed.
There's no escape.

He winces.
I put one hand over his head
and with its thumb
lift his lip
while with the other hand
I poke a brush inside his mouth.
The eye that side half closes.

I squeak the bristles
over canine and molars
then kiss his head.
He licks the taste of toothpaste
from the brush.

I do the other side.

The nights between there's nothing
for him to forgive.

Daramis West

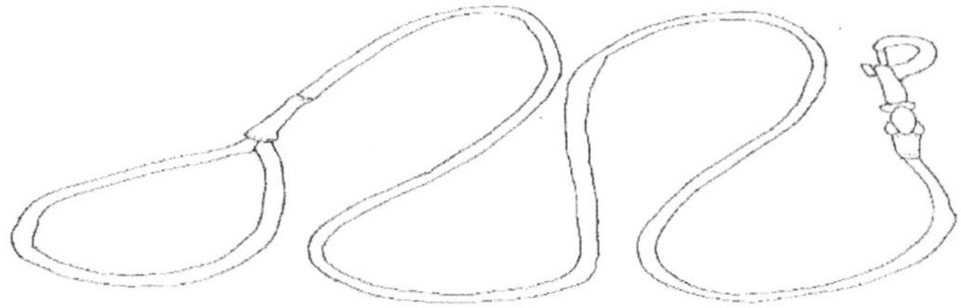

Canal Dog

Hang on a minute, what's the rush?
There's a ripe smell here, no need to push
or pull. Let out the lead, cut me some slack,
take it easy, we'll soon get back.

Learn some patience. I have to wait
while you stop and talk to all your mates.
Light your pipe, clear your throat
talk for ages about your bloody boat.

We don't come along here all that often
where there's bits and pieces nice and soft an'
my pals have walked, left messages for me,
latest news by old elderberry tree.

Fox and badger come at night for a stroll
leave me something in which I can roll.
Shouldn't be ignored nowadays,
few enough, two months of dog days.

You'll get your dinner and I'll be fed
shut in the cabin, sent to my bed.
Another day passed, minimum adventure;
nothing gained as little ventured.

It used to be fun, when Missus was here
but since she's gone there's been little to cheer.
A miserable sod you've turned out to be
passing your melancholy on to me.

Roger Noons

Diggers

First published by Ink Sweat and Tears April 2022

We brought two diggers home,
furious black engines, charged and alive,
fire eyes with a touch of white.

Outside, they clawed the earth,
ripped back its skin, made visible
its bones, a kingdom of limpet arms,

divorced fingers outlining tales
in tongues of dust across the canvas
of the cold travertine noce.

The wind pressed hard that day,
and the sky, seeping ink-rich thick
and slow, emerged along the edge

of tight held lips on broken ground.
But now the earth is smooth,
flat, ironed, surface clean,

and we talk again, imagining
their next act, an outline of our lives
sure to be revealed

in the magician hands of early spring.

Marcello Giovanelli

Dinkie

Otherwise known as Little Man,
he would join in our conversations,
looking knowingly from one to the other.
He would always have the last word when being told off,
making it difficult for us to hide our laughter.
If we had been out for a meal,
he would come bounding to the front door,
for his doggie bag.
If no doggie bag, a black nose would eventually appear
'What time do you call this?' and disappear back to bed.
On Christmas Day we joined forces
with two girl dog-neighbours and their owners.
Naturally there were doggie presents under the tree.
Dinkie couldn't wait for the guests to arrive,
so helped himself to his own present from under the tree.
His party trick was a sitting jump onto the garden table.
He was half Jack Russell half Border Collie
but in a mad moment I told the other neighbours
he was crossed with a mountain goat.
Was it my fault that they believed me?

Anne Hastings

Dog Years

Dogs have marked my childhood, my teenage and adult years
they've known my deepest secrets, shared laughter and my tears.
A long slow walk to clear my head, a broken heart to mend
accompanied all the way, with a four-legged friend.

A Collie through my early years, Jack Russell when I reached ten
a German Shepherd guarding me, when dating strange young men,
then I moved on from my parents' house, got married, but I found,
I was forever lonely, so I got myself a hound.

A dog. I called him Tippy. Loved him with all my heart
and when my marriage floundered, and we decided that we'd part
I got myself another. Not a man. I mean a dog.
My lifeline in the evenings, my early morning jog.
Caring for my animals, gave me a lot to do
my home was never empty. Not one wagging tail, but two.

A Samoyed dog named Shadow, who barked each day at one

to ask if lunch was ready, and if not, well, get it done.
A Greyhound pup, my Polly, from ten weeks my special
friend,
I had her for fourteen years, and when I lost her in the end
I felt my world had come apart, I grieved and couldn't eat
then heard about a homeless dog, I couldn't wait to meet.
My Dusty Dog, a beauty, Saluki cross in cream
nervous, aloof and delicate, we make a special team.

I've loved and lost great people, had awful times as well
but my dogs have helped me cope with them, dragged me
up from Hell.
Have nuzzled me through illness, been there through thick
and thin.
I really wouldn't want a life that had no canine in.

Helen Somers

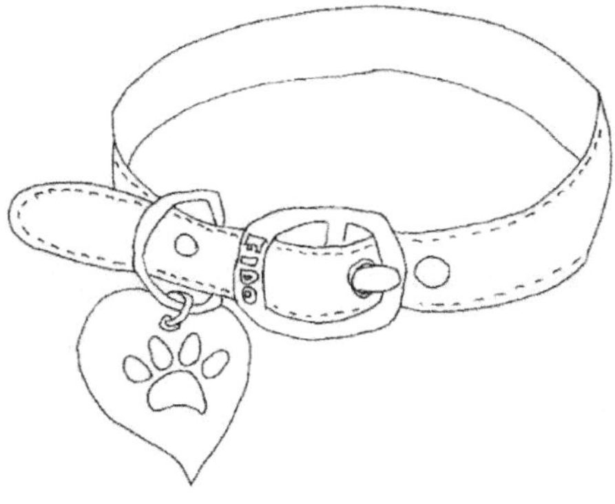

Dolly

Dolly the doggy comes to tea
all for the company of her and me
some nice little treats and a bit of pig's ear
day after day, year after year

Dolly the doggy awaits at my door
through the rain and sunshine, never unsure
and always at the same time, 5pm
and golly she is such a gentle little gem

Dolly the doggy gives many cuddles
she helps through my physical struggles
I adore the beautiful girl, I love her so
it's always an upset when it's time to go

Dolly the doggy today never turned up
the sadness grew and the worry vamped up
hour after hour, day after day
praying for her to come to me once again

month after month and still no news
about the beautiful Dolly, left no clues
my sadness erupted, I lost all my hope
and I wondered how I ever would cope

then came the afternoon, a familiar sound
at the door, 5pm, had Dolly been found?
I look to my surprise, a baby like Dolly
just as sweet and as pretty and ever so jolly

a man walked up behind with a smile on his face
and he gave me a bag of doggy things with grace
he said Dolly died when she had babies at home
and he wondered if I would like a pup of my own

he'd known how I looked out for Dolly every day
and this was a gift kindly sent my way
I smiled and said yes, my own little Dolly
and I cuddled her tight, my new puppy called Polly.

Shell-Marie

Dot of Life

Happinness alongside my dog:
I will not kiss the river
which is flowing by house
in yellow colour with a brown roof
in old Lynton beautiful town
because I don't want to destroy
the light of the dot of life.

Happiness alongside my dog:
I will not kiss the symbols
in Lynton cemetery
behind the church
dressed in old stones
around dancing raw grasses
and white wildflowers
iron leaves of ancient trees
because I don't want to destroy
the light of the dot of life.

Happiness alongside my dog:
I will not kiss the sky
above the Valley of the Rocks
down to Lynton town
rocks which are whirling
around the blue sea

which dance in humanity's
perfect storm
storm of infinite and storm
of death's butterflies
because I don't want to destroy
the light of the dot of life.

Happiness alongside my dog:
I will kiss all of these in my dream, with my voices
rivers, symbols, sky, rocks, grass, flowers
because I want to conserve the mortal
in immortal
in an infinite of universal soul
because I live, I live
in the light of the dot of life
with vocalizing dance in my mind
and happiness alongside my dog.

Lucia Daramus

At the River – Four-Paws and Me

Dog-led to the river,
slip-sliding in mud –
before us a cobbly
ghost riverbed,
riven with rocks
the island awaits…

feral foliage abounds,
a million mirrors
shimmer, sparkle
the water sussurates.

Four-Paws smashes, splashes,
ripples re-arranges, ricochets
into diamond showers of
necklaces spraying upwards,
a mermaid's dowry
the island beckons…

We forage
Four-Paws and me, treasure-seekers,
stick-bearers,
grass and berry-eaters.

On the bank
toes dabbling,
pink tongue lapping,
sitting side by side,
haunch to hip,
fur to skin,
sun-dappled.

Alyson Rhodes

Little Puppy's First Walk

for U.L. and little R.

We made no more than ten steps
when we had to stop.
You always stop when you find something wonderful,
don't you?
Something never-seen-before,
something truly amazing and endlessly admirable.
Something that makes you gasp.

The puppy found exactly such a thing.
The find looked exquisite
with its magnificent colours
and delicate shape –
a little gem in the vast universe,
one of the world's marvellous treasures.
What a thrill to have bumped into it –
a yellow-and-orange blown-down-by-the-breeze
autumn leaf.

Tetyana Lunyova

Little White Canine

Little white canine
fluffy little friend of mine
waiting for me after a long hard day
part Poodle, part Maltese
running
jumping
eager to play
soaking up sun's rays
squeaky toys, with which I heard you love to play.
Seeing you every day puts a smile on that face of mine.
You always make my day!
Little white canine
you truly are a ray of sunshine!

Mary Schmitz

Me and My Dog

Today was a good day we've been over the park,
the sun was shining we did have a lark.
I went on a mission and sniffed everywhere,
nose to the ground
tail in the air.
Mum's feet were hurting
so it's only fair,
we make our way home
we'll take the longest way there.
I'll lay myself down
in the place I like best
Mum puts her feet up and we'll both have a rest.
Today was a good day
it didn't even rain.
Today was a good day
let's do it again.

Evelyn Clare

Mitch – My Scottish Boy (Knock Hill)

I wish you were here; it's not the same without you.

The arterial path is still here, with its veins of sheep tracks

criss-crossing the ankle-high purple carpet of heather

I am not as sure footed as you on the loosened earth,

with protruding rocks, lying in quiet ambush, for my feet

the terrain for you was effortless: you were born for this.

The hill still rises steeply, its scents intoxicating; to me a

gentle, caressing aroma, to you, they assaulted your nose,

causing you to run helter-skelter; tongue lolling; investigating

returning happily once solved, to my outstretched hand

to me the questions remained unanswered and bewildering.

It was your world. I miss you; my hand now only meeting air.

My breathing becomes rapid and my chest tightens, as

I reach the last ascent; but not you; your heart beat,

remained steady and constant; you were bred for this.

Tail swishing; you would wait for me to catch up

it was a game we played. The memory causes me to smile.

Reaching the top, I am rewarded by a 360° view, as vast

as the 360° devotion you opened out to me. The Moray Firth,

Speyside, the moorland of Braemar and the coast of the North Sea

we'd been to them all together, when everything was fresh and new.

It's not the same without you, I wish you were here.

Following tradition, I place a loose rock upon the cairn

this year, I choose a second one for you. Side by side,
in obedience; like our bond unbreakable.

Descending the hill, I feel I am leaving you

further and further behind and the tears fall.

As I click the gate shut, from whence I started

I say goodbye, for I shall never climb that hill again.

Jan Hedger

My Constant Support

My first furry friend was Lassie, a Collie cross by breed
she was always there for me, in my time of need
she'd meet me at the bus stop but one day when running late
we ran and crashed together, I ended in a state
fallen down and broken thumb, in a lot of pain
she licked and whimpered in distress, was never late again.

I then got a Whippet, Tarka, black, a lot of fun
people tried to buy him, when they saw him run
he loved to play at football, his dribbling skills a dream
so that all the players wanted him in their own team
a little thief, he'd steal an apple, eat it but leave the core
the evidence for all to see, he'd left it on the floor.

Brandy, a German Shepherd, when I had a bath
he'd jump in in front of me, it used to make me laugh!
I never put him on a lead, trained him to walk to heel
he lived for eleven years, he'd be a dog to steal.

Snowy was with me, for twelve happy years
he was my little smiler, he'd help me through my tears
he showed no illness, and no pain, I took him to the vets
to have a cyst removed from his tiny neck
the first day of Lockdown, the nation all confused
my heart broke, when she told me, she had terrible news

he had cancer in his lymph nodes, and he was put to sleep
he died in my arms, and all I could do was weep.

I now share my world with another Westie called Sonny
he's the light of my life, cheerful and funny
he knows all his toys, his colours, can talk
and greets me each morning with his belly walk.

Through my life, my dogs have been a constant friend
they never betrayed me, stayed with me till the end.

Jennie Mitchell

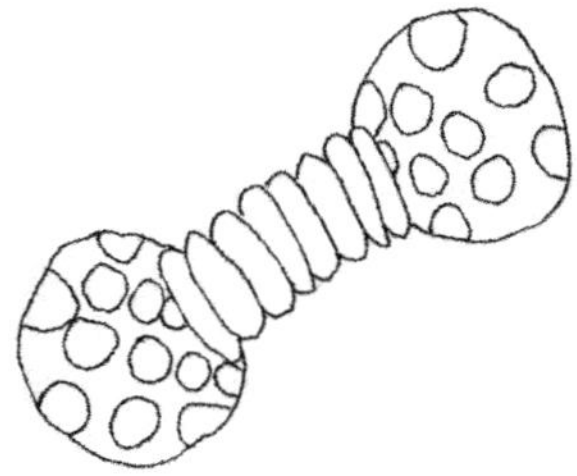

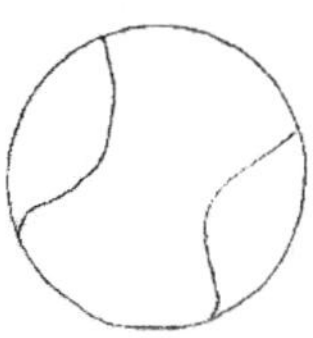

My Dog Galileo

My dog Galileo, snuffling through fallen leaves,
is seeking the source of a scent.
It trails, swirls, maypoles around him.
Nose to the ground, he circles and calculates,
measures, assesses.
Not even a trace by this bole or those roots.
The thread has got broken. He almost despairs.
But it's suddenly there,
knotted and certain, definite, proven:
he's chanced on the spot,
the exact spot
where the squirrel climbed into its tree.

Damaris West

November Night In

5th November
THAT time of year.

It's in full swing
next door's BBQ
sky-high bonfire
rockets fly
Catherines wheel
sparklers sparkle.

Paws over ears time for canines.

Cold out there
but here indoors we're toasty
cosy
Rover and me
chillin' with Mozart
food for the soul
our kind of rock 'n roll.
We play it loud
drowning out the bangs
the whoosh of rockets
Roman candles.

Clock ticks

flames lick the chimney.

Behind closed curtains

we're in good company

Just Mozart

Rover

Me.

Daralyn Hammond

Of Dogs and Men

I had seen him a few times
walking over by the tree line across the way,
it was mostly in the morning
or late afternoon when the
sun cast its long shadows.

Perhaps he had got loose or was
just a stray.
He was a big dog, handsome in his own way,
light brown with four white paws.
Always alert ears and nose held high.
I never had a dog,
I never wanted one,
you see as a kid
I was chased home by a
neighbor's dog.
All I can remember was those snaring teeth
and me screaming for help.
I guess the old saying rings true
'Once bitten twice shy.'

These thoughts played out in my mind
as I filled the food and water bowls.

Opening the screen door
I set my offering down,
the dog's brown eyes met mine
and a sense of understanding prevailed
as he ate and drank.

He was ever alert
watching as my hand touched his scruffy fur.
A strange thing happened, he licked my hand
as if a sign of peace.
I was right, about dogs as well as men.
They won't go away
once fed.

David Painter

A Song for Trudy

Down at the rescue kennels you chose us
a brindle Boxer picked up off the streets
bony ribbed and dark pleading eyes
eyes which hooked me in.
Take me home they said.
Please please take me home.
And we did.

So Trudy girl, we'll sing your song
as you start to settle in.
Your ribs no longer visible
no more need to raid the bin.
And true to Boxers everywhere
you're the joker of the pack.
You can explore the kitchen floor
entirely on your back.

Your zest for life's infectious
you've become a joy to know,
whether bouncing through the young spring corn
or circling in the snow.
The dirtiest of puddles
is your chief delight,

and your snores out on the landing
a comfort blanket in the night.

The children I once cuddled
now all work in distant lands
and a phone call or an email's not the same.
But your muzzle on my knee
reassures me,
that while others come and go
you will remain.

Pauline Hawkins

Rescue Greyhound Racer

She's a marvel, as wonky as
a curly carrot, a two breasted tattie

a gnarled ancient, a crooked house
a squinty eye, a mad professor

rickety ladders, a Budgie playing Subbuteo
a Parrot who thinks he's human

a Pug in love with a cat, snow on Midsummer's Eve
pineapple on pizza, an owl's head swivel

and as weird as birds who see more colours than us
lizards running on water, Ibex Goats on vertical slopes

immortal jellyfish, regenerating Axolotls
Chameleons and dragonflies' eyes rotating 360 degrees

Mimic Octopus shapeshifting into a jellyfish
dolphins sleeping with half their brain awake

the Blue Whale's call at one hundred and eighty-eight decibels
Warblers predicting storms and dogs, cancer in humans.

Maggie Mackay

Rescued

She walks beside me, her soft paws
glide across the snow-covered path,
unaware of the slippery ice that checks
the progress of those with antique knees
and unsteady ankles.

Young, energetic and yet, with every footprint,
she stays with me. Tail up, eyes down,
she searches one side, then the other,
without leaving my side. Not once,
not even for a single step.

She is Dazzle, the rescue dog I released
from behind the iron bars of the rescue centre.
She was barely a month, a pup, but she knew
to poke her tiny black nose through the gap,
to fill the gaps in my suffocating loneliness.

The morning sky turns butter-gold. Sunlight
clears the last of the frozen darkness
as the tip of her tail taps my thigh
to remind me she is here, beside me
to share this moment.

She is Dazzle, my companion, my friend,
my buddy, who walks beside me every day.
The rescue dog I rescued,
who rescued me back.

Kevin Brooke

Runt of the Litter

I cannot hold you
in my hand,
but I know there is light
beneath your tender skin,
a heartbeat resembling
the murmur of an angel.
All it takes is a dampened coat
to expose your fragility:
the raw pinkness of your nose,
the concave edifice of your bones,
legs which shrink into wizened stems.
And you are born again,
runt of the litter.

Laid bare to the light too late,
the last to be exiled
from this cavern of warm bodies,
the final paws to graze
the bloodied ground.
Your mother cannot look
at you for too long
for she must tend to the others.
How many there really are,

she has lost count.
Yet, when your snowy head falls
on her chest as you sleep,
and your tail is tucked somewhere
between her legs,
she smiles inwardly
for you have kept her warm
when the others did not.
She cannot tell you this,
but she was once too
born late, loved little
the runt of the litter.

Iona Mandal

Birmingham Young Poet Laureate 2022-2024

Shadow

My white furred friend
pads behind me.
In the dark, he's a light;
a candle in the night.

He stays close,
licks at my heels
steps his bear like paws in time
with mine.

Slower now,
steady.

Moon clouds wash over his eyes,
age casts its line,
reaches for him,
but he is mine.

My Shadow,
my friend,
the one to whom
I never had to pretend.

Always a teeth bared grin,
a loving face.
A blanket in the cold
        a paw that's always there to hold.

We walk,
my Shadow and I,
we walk
until it's time to say
                goodbye.

Claire Hughes

Song for a Spaniel

A dog is for life
not just for Christmas they say.
Not true, I miss you.

Jane King

Spirit Animal

I'm pulled two ways at least;
Leo is my sign, a bold maned head.

An August birthday
names me a summer baby,
a post war boomer too,
generous as the sun
on a green varnished lochan,
roar flooding the glen
from a dry riverbed.

I'm a sleepy daydreamer,
lazy, whisking my tail all day,
protector of my territory,
unforgiving under duress.
Beware. My bite, my claws finish you off.

But then there's the Collie in me;
squint-glint. I can go on and on all day,
no matter what, born to do a job,
to please my boss, the shepherd.
Crouching bounce.
I'm my poet's familiar,
gold, tan, pepper flecks and flicks.
Careful, I nip and growl.

Maggie Mackay

The Empty Space

Good times we share
a friendship rare
our time ran out
none left to spare.

My heart you wear
a love laid bare
now all I have:
your empty chair.

Gwen Roberts

Together on the Green

He likes to sit upon my lap
and stare beyond those passing
as they perambulate the park
across its pristine, manicured lawns

it calms him,
                    it really calms him.

My hand careless in his fur
across his troubled frown
holding that bantam body close
a tremor to that hot little tail
blown in a subtle wind of his own devising

it calms him,
                    it slowly calms him.

He likes to lay his head upon my legs
and watch the ladies with their prams
as they while away for a while
amidst the ducks, bees and the sometimes breeze
he watches,
                    my thumb circling his ear,

it calms him,
                    it simply calms him.

Jim Jepps

Treasured Tinker Tales

Tinker was a much- loved family dog of the Staffordshire Bull Terrier breed,

whose beloved owner was soon to be joining the WAFS, and whose adoption she had to concede.

And, yes, he had lived in the borough of Staffordshire itself, in a picturesque village near Kinver Edge,

familiar with the countryside air and it's grassy long walks, a devotion with little hesitation to pledge.

His mistress was my grandfather's boss,

it was with heavy heart that they would consider their loss.

Knowing my mother and her sister to be lovers of nature the boss called my grandfather aside and enquired,

my aunt favoured the idea of caring for a dog, but a large canine was to what she would initially have aspired.

A lover of all creatures, but if had been questioned, and to be fair,

would initially have given little consideration to a dog with legs resembling a Queen Anne chair.

Hazel first walked him to the local post office one day where unbeknown to Tinker inside was a lengthy queue, once emerged he had emitted such a sigh of relief, perhaps pondering as to what would become of me without you?

My aunt's measure of devotion was heightened from that day,

to this concerned looking dog and his loyal way.

The rich tapestry of lives soon became intertwined,

with a love and understanding that could not be undermined.

My grandfather would never begin his evening meal without first proffering Tinker some treat from his plate,

whatever was offered he just would not touch before hearing the words 'good dog,' which would cancel out 'wait.'

One evening, when tired, such command slipped his mind, and in fact he just did not think,

only next morning, and upon speaking the words, would Tinker consume his untouched tea drink.

He formed a close bond with Sarah Churchill, the family cat, whom he came to love most dear,

upon sleeping, the cat's movements were dictated by his as he later developed chorea.

In subsequent years he would listen for the local Round Oak Steel Work's one o'clock sound, and at this my mom would worry,

he would leave what he was doing in order to meet my mom from work nearby, oblivious to traffic, and eager to hurry.

A grocery van had become a local street visit, and also customer, a Mrs Baggott,

of whom I am certain would never forget,

Tinker's distinctive greeting, that of finding her legs warm and wet.

Of becoming a family top dog pet, he had made the graduation,

upon being buried by my grandfather on a warm summer's day I heard it said that tears of sadness were intermingled with those of perspiration.

Many years later, in a graduation photograph taken with my mom, Hazel made an unexpected comment that if you almost closed your eyes, we had disappeared, ordinarily without reason, or rhyme,

seemingly highlighting a vision of Tinker, their dog, transcending an image in time?

Laura Louise Reynolds

True North

My dog's true north is every dog in view.
Attracted like a lodestone to its pole,
he swerves and spins to keep his magnet true,
his will in perfect concert with his soul.

Not until the avenue we walk
descends a curve that hides his avid goal
does he decide to quit his stubborn balk
and pay heed at last to his owner's scold.

A paragon of purpose on four paws,
he demonstrates the qualities I lack;
an eagerness to attack a threat of jaws
or beaks, a fearless shield before or aft,
while, shackled to my self-held leash of doubt,
I conjure more anxieties to sprout.

John Newsom

Two Black Dogs

I have one black dog that loves me
I have another who thinks I'll fail always
one black dog adores me
the other feels a different way.

One black dog gives me freedom
one black dog gives me chains
one block dog is my companion
the other might drive me insane.

One black dog shares my adventures
the other locks me inside
one will be with me whatever, whenever
the other black dog makes me hide.

One black dog always has a lick for me
the other more likely to kick me down
one black dog who will bring me his toy
the other would lead me to drown.

One black dog shares warmth with me
the other an oppressive dead weight
one shows me unconditional love

the other dog triggers self-hate.

Both black dogs I feed
only one of them shows love to me
one I give toys and bones to chew
the other gets my self-doubt and negativity.

Both dogs rarely leave my side
never going too far away
one faithfully keeps me safe
the other lets me go astray.

One black dog is my soulmate
we operate as one being
the other black dog is more of a curse
that sends my confidence fleeing.

One black dog I would never choose to be without
the enabler, the faithful, the hero
the other black dog I'd love to go away
when he lingers I am zero.

Everyone loves my one black dog
with him I am a better human being
no one can see the other black dog

though he is huge and full of negative feeling.

You see, I have two dogs, not one
both are as black as night
but one shines like a beacon to me
and helps me with my fight.

The other? Well I try to ignore him
though I don't always succeed
over that black dog I seek mastery
to keep on a shortened lead.

My one black dog is beloved
my soldier in the war I fight each day
I treasure him despite his rebellious quirks
and he keeps the other black dog at bay.

Blind Johnny Smoke

Two Months, Four Days, Twenty-One Hours

I no longer hear the jingle
of snaps and buckles
on my old dog's coat
as he tried to stand
to ask for help.

I no longer hear the whisper
of fur and blankets
as my old dog shifted
in the bed he rarely left
at the end.

Now I see calla lilies everywhere—
the bloom he brought to me in a dream—
reminding me to listen
to the jingle and the whisper
in my soul.

Helen Zax

Two-Gether

Westie Vicky, sails my father's chest
rising and falling with each breath.
Their choir of snores accompanies
TV's endless Emmerdale and Corrie.

Later, paws hearthed, she gazes
into flames that tiger heat and light,
seeing gravy coated turkey giblets
and crustless soldiers dipped in egg.

Four, splat paws take turns to twitch.
Fleet as Hermes, Vicky runs her dreams,
seeks butterflies, rabbits and cats
and captures every fleeing one.

A wrapper rustles and an ear quivers.
Is it a favourite, silver-papered Polo
or a cellophane wrapped toffee?
Man and dog drool their anticipation.

They await supper timed for News at Ten.
In tune, both perk at Big Ben's bongs.
Time to share crackers and cheese

and tea from Dad's blue striped mug.

Their worlds always revolve as one,
little fingers and dewclaws entwined.
Hearts and tums perfectly matched,
one man and his dog are one.

Gillian Scholey

Walking in the Rain

Thumb trigger-ready
locking the leash
keeping snout
from crumbs, saving
a good ploatin'
from the huge pup
approaching.

We lurch at the ball-of-hair
Questioning
our energy provider.

I have to say
on a better day
I'm more polite
to the pinnied youth
bouncing around my
feigned intrigue
at the steamed shop
windowpanes

feet and paws
skim the flagstones
as we skitter quick
getaways.

Julie Meredith

Wellington

Passing on the train
through the station with your name
I noticed a fellow passenger
cradling a tiny fair puppy in their lap
and it takes me back to when we first met
and you were that small
a minute bundle of over-excitement
with a chaotic curiosity
an energetic urge to explore
this wondrous world you found yourself part of.
Sniffing out new smells in the delightful garden,
gallivanting across grass, bounding round bushes
to a bright green patch you haven't seen before
and you leap onto it
then stop
then flounder
something is not right
where is the solid ground you expected?
Beneath your paws
there is only wet stuff
you start to sink.

Of all the people there, I was first to react
to leap forward and grab you
scooping you out of the water
wiping away the pond weed
I'm handed a towel, so I wrap you in it
gradually drying you off
cradling you, tiny fair puppy, in my lap.

Alison Manning

Who Rescues Whom?

(a Haiku):

I won't be lonely
during my retirement –
rescued by rescue.

Dominic Willis

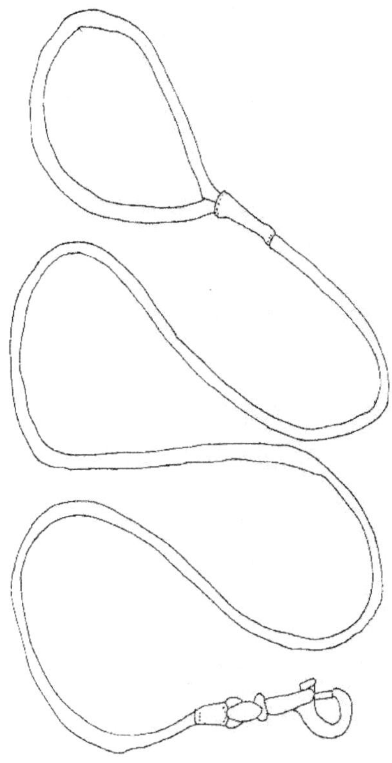

Wolf Moon, Last Night

For Percy Dog, lost 30th October 2023

They will say I was dreaming and look at me with pity, while implying I must have been mistaken. They will say I'm overwrought, stricken with grief, and the grieving mind plays tricks. They will tenderly insist I was only half awake, in that space between consciousness and sleeping, and helpfully suggest I should see my GP for something to help me get some rest. They will likely put it down to my wild imagination, which, to be fair, is often unruly. They will say I felt what I wanted to feel which was, after all, natural enough. But I will shake my head. I will not be persuaded because I know I was awake and you came to me. I felt the weight of you curled against me, pressing against my legs. Then, eyes closed, but most definitely awake, I repeated your name like a prayer. It was then I felt the rapid beating of your tail. You were excited, telling me hello. I cried a little. I was sad but happy. I was comforted because I knew you were with me. I began to feel sleepy so I dried my eyes and settled on my side with a sigh. But – oh how wondrous! – you moved in my arms. I was aware of your energy pulsating. Your presence, unmistakeable, fluttered like a heartbeat as I held you in the hollow of my arms. Wolf Moon last night, bright as a promise. Three moons have waxed and waned since I lost you. But last night, you and I, we snuggled up close and I felt your breath on my cheek.

Abigail Ottley

Zoomies

Our dog enters the house
with glee. Rescued, now
she rescues me. This beast
found matted and with fleas
now gives a sense of family.
She knows who's welcome
in the pack and curls her
body in the back
behind our knees as we lay
down. She is a joy to
have around. How often
do we zoom around?
Unleash the joy of
being found? Run around
our chosen home
to celebrate our safe
return. How much we
have to learn from her
this little bit of bark
and fur.

Elizabeth Tessier

PART FOUR

WORKING DOGS

After Boadie (My Retired Hearing Dog)

I've taken up your bed
and put it back again;
that space on the floor was all wrong.
In the dark of night I tread carefully
around where you used to lay.

And the old rainbow beach towel
that I dried you with after a rainy walk,
that's still on its hook.
And talking of hooks,
the ones by the back door,
your leads are still there.

My pockets are full of treats
and in the car boot, there's your duvet
and that posh bedspread,
the one you sprawled on
like a Sultan.

I miss your whiskery face
and the comfort of your old body
against my leg.

Maggie Hampton

Amazing Henry

Gorgeous Henry are you
A sponsor dog for me
I am so so happy too
You are beautiful you see
Soft and cuddly you are
Proud to show you off
You even like the car
You don't even mind my cough
We are a team you and me
Places we go all over to see
Together and happy as can be
In shops on buses is he
I love you so much
You make my day
You are so lovely to touch
Soft and fluffy here to stay
Thanks to all for giving me you
I am so grateful and caring
We are so happy us two
Thank you so much for sharing.

Elizabeth Watkinson

Dogs With Jobs

I'm thinking of applying – for a different sort of job
generally performed by a Border Collie breed of dog
at least that's what I thought, until I looked it up
but for dog detection jobs, they use various kinds of pup.

They do use German Shepherds but usually for outdoor tasks
useful during covid, as they didn't have to wear those masks
there are dogs from Czechoslovakia and the Belgian Malinois
or the Labrador Retriever, the calmest dog by far.

There are lots of European dogs, within the detection mix
and feel though I am human, I could perform many sniffing tricks
all that I would need to seek any smuggled items out
is my fine honed sense of smell and super sensitive kind of snout.

I'd not want to be a Cadaver Dog, searching out human remains
rather fly to exotic places to run round airports or on planes
the world would be my oyster, though I hope not to detect faeces
prefer to prevent importation of rare endangered species.

I'm often smelling smells, other humans can't detect
but doin' all this sniffin' really makes me feel quite wrecked
on a discriminatory basis my application may just fail
due to my lack of heavy panting and the absence of a tail.

Jo Vick

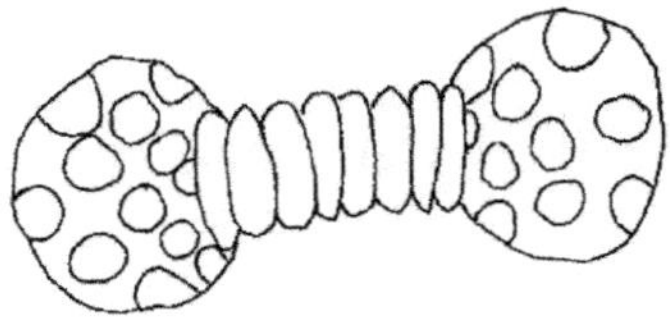

Finding Ifton Quarry

We found a new path today;
the way through the woods to Ifton Quarry.
It took some finding.
Beyond a barbed wire fence,
the old limestone quarry was wreathed
in shadows. Danger, said the signs.
Keep Out.

Sid, in his element, dashed ahead
all a-caper, then waited, impatient,
round the next corner.
He cared nothing for the barbed fence
or the quarry's ghosts, spannelling
into the forbidden ground and back.
Quick, quick!
Burrs tangled in his woolly coat,
but what did it matter?
This wood, this path, this moment…
All ours.

Maggie Hampton

Following

The shepherd wends his way back to the farm
his dogs have done their labour for the day.
The sheep are safe within the fold, but yet
the darkness overtakes them on the way.

A white tail wags ahead on the dark path,
no lantern needed as they find their way.
The Spaniel knows the way to reach their home
and brings them safely back to close the day.

Elizabeth Falding

Historically hill farming shepherds often kept a white-tailed Spaniel along with their sheepdogs. After dark they would all follow the wagging white tail home. These dogs were often nicknamed 'lantern dogs'.

Guide Dog

A young man called Ross who was not able to see from birth.

Only with family fighting get a Guide Dog for young son

which they won.

Now Ross is able to be more independent with new Guide Dog called Sue.

It's amazing how has transform Ross's life.

Sue is Ross's eyes.

Ross had a surprise for best friend Sue; he bought a toy now

which brought so much to Sue.

Ross and Sue were busy every weekend

now Ross less dependent his family

Sue and Ross had built amazing friendship

Sue helps Ross get to work.

Ross was a school teacher at a primary school near home.

Sue helped Ross get around the school.

The children in Ross's class knew she was working her yellow harness on.

As time went on,

Ross and Sue brought great joy each lives

now the possibilities are endless. Ross now Sue his helping hand.

Sue and Ross would keep him getting lost.

Sue was member Ross family

everywhere Ross went Sue everyone knew them.

Ross needed Sue to help pursue his dreams.

Ross wanted to do a sponsored walk to help raise money for the charity that helped Ross to get his Guide Dog called Sue.

Ross was a true inspiration to other people with sight loss.

Ross gave some earnings to the Guide Dog charity.

Ross and Sue were able to go on holidays around UK.

Now that Ross had Sue this left Ross's family to worry about.

Ross and Sue were able to do whatever Ross needed to do.

Ross asks himself how different life would have without Guide Dog Sue and they were each best friends

as Ross knew depends on his Guide Dog to help anything that young man needs to do.

Jay Joshi

Have You Seen My Ears?

Have you ever seen a dog that listens for a living?

Who's on alert from night 'til day, no really I'm not kidding!

Have you heard about the dog who listens to the wind,

who wonders 'Is that a noise, I should be checking in?'

Do you know of such a dog who makes note of every sound,

and knows which one to work for, who's ever duty bound?

How about that four pawed pal that sleeps right by the bed,

forever at the humum's side no matter where they rest their head.

Have you ever seen a dog that listens for a living?

Eager eyes, shiny nose and a heart forever giving.

Well take a look just to my left and tell me what you see,

that's not just any dog, that's the better part of me!

Maxine Clare

Hill Sheep Faith

We soon lose our path in snow.
Confetti of unhappiness

gathers the crows to feast.
Mishaps will happen up here,

but hear our protector's bark.
We trudge for lower ground,

share warmth, we flock as one.
We hear the bark. All are safe.

Phil Wood

Loneliness

It's a sense of grief for what I used to know,
a knot in my stomach that won't ever go.
It's feeling unworthy and stuck in one place,
whilst everyone moves at a much faster pace.
It's feeling alone in a room full of chatter,
missed conversations but, it's ok, 'it doesn't matter.'
It's saying no to things yet feeling left out,
many missed moments, overwhelming self doubt.
It's being around friends where I laugh and smile,
this mask is exhausting but I'll be home in a while.
It's saying, 'I'm good, thanks,' to others who care,
feeling a burden, unable to share.
It's sleeping in until the afternoon,
just a few more hours, it will be bedtime soon.
It's coming home to my hiding place,
but what happens when that no longer feels safe?
It's a glimmer of hope in the still of the night,
and holding on to that small piece of light.
It's meeting your sweet, four paws for the very first time,
so loving, not judging, pinch me, are you mine?
It's whispering into your soft, floppy ears,
I feel anxious today, I'm so glad you're here.
It's walking together on a journey for two,

looking ahead and starting anew.
It's no longer feeling like I need to hide,
I'm building confidence with you by my side.
It's being completely myself with you,
not wanting to change or be someone new.
It's having you here and feeling secure,
I no longer feel alone anymore.

Lucy Higgins

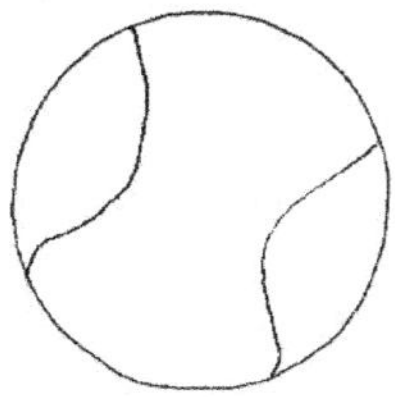

Old Bess

Old Bess was never mine at heart,
though it was I who spoke breath into her
when she was born, the last of six,
an awkward, scrappy, tremble of a pup.

By day and night I coaxed and coddled her
with warmth and hourly drops of milk.
For weeks all else was set aside
to kindle life in her and love in me.

Her siblings sold, but no one wanted Bess,
by then a quavering, skinny, homely beast.
But time and love proved every mocker wrong,
for she grew best who started out as least.

Good fare soon strengthened her unsteady legs;
good care stirred courage in her timid mind.
This much is true, I gained her lifelong trust,
but no, her love was never mine to keep.

To me she came for food and evening walks,
to me she gave affection and respect;
but Border Collies crave a shepherd's touch

and it was John who won her sheepdog heart.

Alert to every whistle, every call,
each Steady, Come Bye, Hold, Away, Lie Down,
her cheek she rested on the shepherd's knee,
her loving gaze she fixed on John alone.

Arrow straight to rescue wandering sheep
or weaving like a shadow through the flock,
shepherd, sheepdog, lived and worked as one
until the Master Shepherd called John home.

Resisting any other shepherd guide,
Bess grieved for John until the day she died.

Rhona Stephens

Shepherding

High

fells,

Herdwicks

are rounded

'come-bye', 'away', 'stand',

working dogs, shepherding commands,

circling, steering, controlling with quick synchronised paws,

in unison, straying Herdwicks

gathered soundly, heart-

racing, hooves

pounding,

job,

done

Susan Wood

Sunshine

When I first met you, I was drawn to your lovely brown eyes!
You remind me of a cuddly teddy bear!
Your delicate face so beautiful and mischievous
especially when you bound into my home...

Your eyes dart around
and I know you are looking for my shoes
so you can remove and run off with my insole
like you have with my heart.

You run around the room this way and that,
watching me
as if you are saying 'catch me if you can!'
Just like a young child!

Your tight black curls, soft like a lady's luxurious coat, the envy of all who shop.
When you see me in the street I smile
and so do those around as you dance towards me like a ballerina,
so graceful as you tiptoe on your two back feet!

What joy you give us as you look after Mel so well
filling her with security and love.
Our beautiful Kirrie!

Patricia D. Wardle

Taking the Silence Away

Two years of training,
a long waiting list and
today's the day an assistant
has been assigned to me.

After our first five hours
together, he has taken
the silence away,
I am able to breathe again
without feeling ashamed.

His gentle eyes carefully follow me,
his paws carefully make contact with my body,
his ears become my ears,
we speak a language
we both understand.

When I see him,
when I feel him,
when I need him,
I call him, and he hears me,
when he talks,
I can hear him.

Adriana Rocha

When Silence Falls

There may come a time when silence falls
for those who live alone, and nobody calls,
with no one else to alert when someone is at the door,
or walking inside, who are they and what are they here for?

The bell may ring but I don't know if someone is there,
the visitor may not be visible and wander around somewhere.
Then one day I received a young companion,
a Hearing Dog I call 'Snoopy,' a worthy champion.

He was a bit lazy at first and would sleep,
until I trained him then he would leap,
and now alerts me at an instance of any noise,
nudging me and standing with composure and poise.

Snoopy welcomed or saw off any stranger at the door,
wagging his tail now aware what he is here for.

Timothy P. Stavert

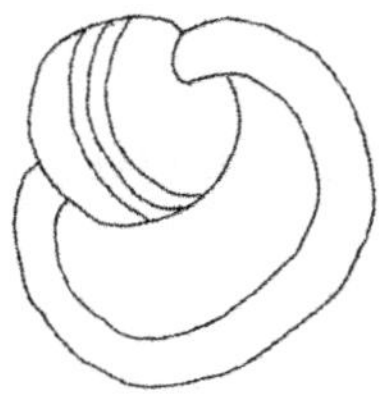

The poems in this collection are written in varieties of English including: British English, American English, and Australian English. Spellings reflect the variety of English used by individual authors. Some poems are written by authors whose first language is British Sign Language, therefore, the grammatical structure of these poems reflects this.

Hearing Dogs for Deaf People

Deafness is rising in the UK; by 2035, it is estimated that one in five British people (over 15 million) will experience hearing loss.

Hearing Dogs for Deaf People is a national charity that trains dogs to alert deaf people to important and life-saving sounds like the smoke alarm, alarm clock and doorbell. Their burgundy coats also act as a visual reminder to the public when they are out and about that their partner is deaf.

Deafness can be a very isolating disability, so a Hearing Dog offers constant companionship and emotional support, giving deaf people the confidence to reconnect with their family, friends and community around them. This combination of practical assistance and lifelong friendship can be completely life-changing.

Charity Website and Messaging

www.hearingdogs.org.uk

Hearing Dogs for Deaf People helps deaf people to leave loneliness behind and reconnect with life.

In support of

Hearing Dogs
for Deaf People

Dream Well Writing Ltd

Dream Well Writing Ltd are Staffordshire based publishers of dyslexia friendly books – with worldwide distribution and an environmentally conscious ethos – founded in 2017 by Mel Wardle Woodend Staffordshire Poet Laureate 2019 – 2022.

Find out more about Dream Well at

http://dreamwellwriting.simplesite.com/

https://www.facebook.com/dreamwellwriting/

dreamwellwriting@gmail.com

Printed in Great Britain
by Amazon

61535801R00088